Midnight Lyrics

To those whose minds never cease

Contents

I. Question Everything

"We have two lives, and the second one begins when we realize we only have one."

- Confucius

She Said Nothing

I told the moon about you
and she said nothing

I shouted silence back
in the form of thoughts
deep like the nights black
swirling cycle of knots

I thought of your arms as blankets
whispering "you are the most
loveliest thing I have ever seen"

I told the moon that
we used to drive for hours talking
dancing like we were in the rain

she knows how we tangled ourselves
together like twine
and watched the stars together
thinking you were mine

what she doesn't know is
how fast you spun me
into a melody of falling stars
beautifully lethal

she never saw the way your eyes
filled when looking at me
she never heard the whispers
atop pillows

I told her how you make me feel
alive because you make me feel

I told her that I miss your words
the same ones that shattered
splitting my heart to thirds
making the hurt seem surreal

I asked her to give me
dreams about you
and if she could
sing them to me

I told the moon
everything about us
of every swoon and burn
but she said nothing in return

why should I?

you will never be
as young as you are right now
* * *
that's why

Zoom Out For a Second

why does no one talk about
how we are floating
on a dirt rock
in space
in the cosmos

we are a carbon based
intellectual
metacognisant species

the odds of that?

when I lay on a hillside
I am rounded by the earth
resting on land
surrounded by water
orbiting a ball of gas

I sit and work as
we are spinning
forever spinning

like waves and currents
there before us
and there way after
we are gone

if it ever stops turning
we would fly off the soil

so here I am
all this time to sleep
this time to write

time to waste
or to fill

all this time to work
on positive thinking and
think positively about work

all this time
to tell you
to wake up

or stay asleep because
we dream of them every night

instead I stare at the ceiling
wondering of everything in between

Loose Leaf

paper means creativity

you can draw
write
fold
scribble
burn
paint
tear
even cry on your paper
the tears will show

we as humans fill that sheet
with ink or lead
ink is my preference
as it rolls smooth
onto the page and
the noise it makes when I
cross my t's

you can make paper airplanes
and have your ink fly
around the room

crumbled paper will
keep a fire going
like how a book can
fuel imagination

paper can fuel a fire like
the paper that
declared our independence

we the people are the fire
burned by the rules that
fueled revolutions and justice

there would be no history
without paper
no stories to read
or paintings to admire

what was once a beautiful

ALIVE tree is now a
DEAD one

'loose leaf'
they call it but
the loose leaves
that fall off the trees
scream for their lives
when they meet the axe

it's ironic how much we take
trees for granted
am I the devil for this book?
for loving the art of the novel?

we forget they provide the
air we breathe
or the paper we write on
or homes to other life

we forget they were
childhood escapades
and shade on a blistering day

we forget to be grateful
because we simply keep
turning the page

Reasons to Stay

a sun-kissed day
after a cold night
the blow of wind
on sweat layered skin
cigarettes
after a night of drinking
those first words
of your favorite song
the wood burning and cracking
the orange and pink painted
sky's of twilight
the taste of you
before bed
seeing you smile
from my words
the first swim of summer
the sound of a river
or pen on paper
first flurry snowfall
first orange leaf
to hit the ground

clear sinuses
when you fall asleep
and dreams
that leave you smiling
your hand
on my cheek and
my legs wrapped in yours

the laughs - all of them

that book
that made me forget the world
that one pen
that writes so perfectly
the morning dew
a blanket and a book
when it rains
a warm bed
when it snows
the last 30 minutes of work
the anticipation of _____
greasy food
when you're drunk

your favorite pair of pants
the last line of a book
and hope
when all else is gone

-the roses do smell good

Eight Eyes

oh to be
a spider
in the corner
perched on
a web
more veiled
than a fly
on the wall

I Asked The Moon Again

like the sun in our sky
I had a burning question
I asked the moon if she knew
of the beginning or end

she does not answer
through words
nor sounds and letters
but through those
who enter our lives
and those who change us
for the better

"will it work out in the end?"
I asked her
no matter day or night
I think she hears me
because she is always there
casting some sort of light

that is the point of it all

not to know our fate
because if we waited
for the outcome
rather than living our call
the time to enjoy it would be too late

II. Sleep When I'm Burned

What if it could turn out better than you imagined?

6 AM

if you never went to sleep
would you consider that a night?

the sun is not awake
a sliver of light
almost due break

sometimes I look into the shade
and see everything
but often I see nothing
which makes me more afraid

the shadow's silence is near
following every move
and thicker darkness is unclear
like it has something to prove

I cannot see beyond
my computer screen
or the words on the page
the only light shinning

the dead scene
or the man cracked with age

my fan runs on setting two
the blades spinning endlessly
my mini fridge sings a tune
about how my head spins
like the blades too

the good ones cry
and the sad ones write
but they don't tell you
the mad ones only write at night

Nocturnal

sometimes I wonder
what life would be like if
we all lived under the stars
and dreamt under the sun
what kind of humans
would we be then?

Dear Insomnia

I push my body a little further
from the bed
as if I am floating

you make me
punch my comforter and
kick the desolate air

you make me run outside and shout
"let me sleep damn you!"
though my brain won't settle
or waste time
forcing itself to sleep
when it could be creating

maybe i'll write a few lines about
how you make me stare at the ceiling
or
how you make me toss my sheets as
if someone else were here

you make me live in a
quiet world
though I only complain a small
amount because I appreciate
the quiet

I appreciate the time alone
the peace
the silence
the time to simply be

Don't Wake Me

I wish
the clouds
would simmer
making the stars
appear
because
the dream
cannot hear
the dreamer

III. Tears Quench The Soul

Beauty comes of all things

Medicine

we each
had a bed
but instead
we lived
in my car
and
we didn't
drive
that far
to end up
dead
but we are
because
there's no good end
to an
addiction

Coping Mechanisms

the tears that fell
for you were the ones that
hit the floor

how many tears
will fall for you?

would I be able to hold
the salty puddle in my hand?
would it fill a tea cup?

if I had counted every single one
would I be able to float
on my back by the current
or would I drown?

how many tears
soaked in my hair
for the days I won't see you again?

how many tears

bonded to my shirt
for not hearing your voice again?

how many tears
dripped from my chin
for never feeling your hands again?

how many fell
for the days we had and
the days we won't get to have?

how many dropped for love
and how many for hate?
how many tears
didn't come from being too numb?

how many tears have fallen
trying to let you go?

how many more will fall
because I did
and how many more
because you didn't

Red

the color of blood
    of the flags I walked passed
to get to you
    of my eyes when you said it
was for the best
    of the chocolate wrappers I
never threw away
    of the liquor cap trying to
    forget your name
    and you
as my red herring

A Kiss of Light and Anguish

pain isn't just a stubbed toe
on the corner of a table
it's not just that foul feeling of
dread and fear
it's not just the sting of the wound

pain is a canvas, spilled with ink

pain is fear and it's also joy
because without despair
there would be no delight
without fear
we wouldn't feel that rush

pain is also a roller coaster
that makes your stomach drop
it's your heart beating out of your
chest and thrumming in your blood
it's your rising temperature
and sweaty palms
it's your every thought

and your next move

we learn in life not to inflict pain by
learning from our mistakes

so don't walk too close
to the table corner
don't allow your heart to be
shattered
careful not to spill the ink
to write your story for you

we learn not to believe
in love at first sight
we learn not to trust
we learn how to deal with stress
because that's all we have anymore

pain is the sore throat
that you can't swallow
pain is dried tears
it's a blank stare and no words
it's a forced smile

it's the noise that cannot be heard

Small Poem

sometimes
I wish the apple
fell further from the tree

Thinking Thoughts

when I write
you are between the lines and
when I read you are
an image in my head

no
I am not paying attention
to my professor talk about
Eliot's *Wasteland*

I agree that summer did
surprise us because
that was when we met and
by the end of it
I knew what the thunder said

even if you were miles away
or pressed to me
there was always a
part of my brain that
consumed you

like the soil consumed
the burial of the dead

The Sun Casts the Likeness of You

I have two shadows
that trail my back
mine and the
memory of you

IV. Mortal Beings

If you think life is short then it will be

A Clock Goes

Strike.
The first hand shortest and the
second hand
      not as fast as the seconds
go by. Twenty four hours in a day
    in a clock
          to do
anything with you. Not enough

time
    in a night to spend watching
the hands go round and ticking,
warning us that time is
         of the
essence.
It's round edges or sometimes flat,
sometimes white or red digital.
    I envy the way the hands
always reset
    thriving off of the electricity
that runs through them, powered by

the sun or triple A batteries or
sometimes powered through motion.
                              Strike
        my wrist if I'm minutes late
        or reverse time
                              if a
mistake.
It never stops, even when it is not
moving, time will never cease
                              to exist
        like the hands never cease
                              to tick.

The Art of Now

our entire life
is a fleeting moment

it's there
it's now
it's here

we try to enjoy
every
damn
second
when we realize
the moments are
all we have

and then they become
nothing more
than a
memory
in the ether

Ephemeral

24 hours too few

not enough minutes in hours
because when we talk
seconds fly by us
faster than arrows

the sun rises and
there is not enough
stars to gaze with you
not many stars
shine brighter than you
when you laugh
a melody of
flowers and blossoms

too few hours
in a day to hear you
your voice like golden silk
your eyes a sea I drown in
flourish in

not enough movies or sunsets
to watch with you
not enough endless days
and sleepless nights
not enough pages in a book
we both fall into

never enough
it will never be enough
but I will take 24 hours
over none

Three Hands on a Clock

two hands point to the twelve
simultaneously waiting

I will try to sleep and
lay my head on
soft salted sheets
woven together with wool
in a glorious knot

I try not
to stare at the clock
on the wall watching
the hands move apart
and together like
two hopeless romantics
attracted to each other
by bliss and burn

the hands now meet
once again at the
three

following each other's
subsequent steps like
fog does above water

like how darkness
covers everything
but light touches
what we want to see
and we see what we covet
because human nature is to covet
and desire love as a fondness
not a function

I wish our hands could
meet together like
the two hands
on the four forever moving
together intertwined by a
pulsating pendulum
beating separate never more

V. The Worth

My thinking of you never ends

Poem

the very thought of you
has my arms wide open
like a book with pages
begging for words

The Alphabet Game

And so we were in my car
Bellowing and giggling and we
Couldn't stop. another
Decade gone by in the blink of one
Eye. the way the
Fun ripples off our
Giant smiles because we are
Here, right now.
Incredibly lucky to have
        found each other
Just in time for living. it
Kicked our asses when we
Laughed till our ribs hurt
Making names and ashes.
Not only can we make the room
        rumble but we are
Over the games and drama, over the
Pretentious bullshit, over the
Questions and rules that
Ruin friendships.
Stand with me now friends. I know

There isn't one of you who would
Underestimate our capability to be
Vulnerable. even
When they can't find a word that
    starts with an
X, we make sure she finds her way.
You guys are the greatest thing to
    happen to me,
        even when we play the game in
        the car from A to
Z

My Eyes

I wish you had my eyes
so you could see

the way your hair curls
around your ears
or the way you light up
at the sound of my voice

you could see your
incandescent smile
bright enough to
light the underworld

the way you pick at your nails
when you are anxious
or when you laugh
with silver in your eyes

I wish you had my eyes
so you could see
the way time stops

when you enter a room
the way you glow
when you talk about your passion

you could see the way your eyes
flutter when you're falling asleep
or feel the way my heart throbs
when you look at me

the way your tears make
your cheeks glisten
or how your lips form the
most beautiful shape

I wish you had my eyes
so you could see
the way you love
and the way you hate

see the way you carry yourself
or the way you fall

the way your skin

changes to my touch
and how your body fits mine
you could see the way I see you
beautiful with no end

if you had my eyes angel
you would see the single most
beloved creature to me

you would never question
your worth or beauty
you would forget you
thought of yourself any less

I wish you had my eyes
so you could see
until then I will try everything
to make you see as my eyes do

The Important Ones

if not
for support
we would
crumble
so slowly
only
our bones
keeping us
upright

Ethereal

our song is strong
like braided silk

our story is deep
like the seas trenches

our connection is ethereal
its like a telepathic embrace
comforting and warm

our art is like burning medal
glowing incandescent blue light
like your eyes do at dawn

VI. Sweet Dreams

*"In dreaming, the clouds methought
would open, and show riches ready to
drop upon me; that, when I waked,
I cried to dream again."*
- *William Shakespeare*, The Tempest

Jokes by Your Subconscious

you were there last night
when I confessed myself bare
you told me
you missed me too
we were happy
I was happy
but
my chest gave way
when I woke to find
it was fake the whole time

Question Everything

is death the portal
to the afterlife?
the entrance to
Dantes *Paradise*
or his treacherous *Inferno?*
is it all blackness and nothing
like it was before?
is it the last and final
pain we feel before
God lets us through the gates
or damns us like Lucifer?
is it the beginning
of something new?
is death really a death at all?
the scariest and most exciting part
is we will never know for sure
until we get there ourselves

Morbid Dreams

one day
I will either be
a
pile of ashes and teeth
inside a metal vase
or
rotten bones inside a coffin
a
bloody pulp
smeared
on the road
or
disintegrated in lava
or
dinner for a beast
or maybe
just maybe
I spit through the sky
to the light
maybe
my spirit flies

so high
I join
the rest of
the stars
burning eternal

Clap Twice for Society

humans are meant
to live in
the sun
but
some live
under the desk lamp
burning
like
our hearts
burn to flee
from its
desk window

Acknowledgments

I want to extend a sincere thank you to those who have helped me form this piece.

To Matthew Kilbane, my poetry professor at the University of Notre Dame, for providing feedback on many of these poems. With your professional help and guidance, I was able to craft my poems to where I wanted them to be. Thank you for being a caring and educational inspiration.

To my friend and fellow writer, Maggie, for being an essential peer reviewer, and helping me with the editing process.

To my dearest friends: Christina, Ashley, Sarah, and Allison for reading and supporting my passion for as long as I can remember. I will never forget my original support team.

To my honest, yet loving sister Luciana, for always hearing every new poem whether she wanted to or not.

To my parents who have supported me throughout this process and never doubted my abilities. Thank you for teaching me that with work and passion, anything is possible. My number one fans always.

To the rest of my friends and family who knew about my goals and encouraged me, your efforts are appreciated in every way.

And to you, the reader. Without you, my dream would never be possible. I hope these poems help you sleep a little better than before.